better together*

*This book is best read together, grownup and kid.

 **akidsco.com**

a kids
book
about

a kids book about RESILIENCE

by Jamie Mustard

a kids book about

Printed in the United States of America.

A Kids Book About books are available online: *akidsco.com*

To share your stories, ask questions, or inquire about bulk purchases (schools, libraries, and nonprofits), please use the following email address: *hello@akidsco.com*

Print ISBN: 978-1-958825-83-9
Ebook ISBN: 978-1-958825-84-6

Designed by Jelani Memory
Edited by Emma Wolf

Images in this book were generated
with the assistance of Midjourney.

This magical book is dedicated to my friend Dr. Jay Faber, and to each and every kid and grownup who is facing what they think might be impossible, and who decides to turn that impossibility into a voyage of learning and possibility.

Intro

Anyone, no matter how big or small, has to deal with things that seem really hard. And sometimes, things that may even seem impossible.

It can feel like you are the only person dealing with that impossible something, but I promise you, EVERYONE, no matter how their life may look, even if easy from afar, eventually encounters something they think just might be impossible. That impossible thing might be a great quest, difficult mission, or other people who make life hard.

This book will present you with a choice. That choice will be how you approach any difficult path in front of you. You can choose to view a hard path as something unbearable or unfair. OR, maybe you approach this road believing it can take you on the greatest adventure of your life!

This book is too hard to read.

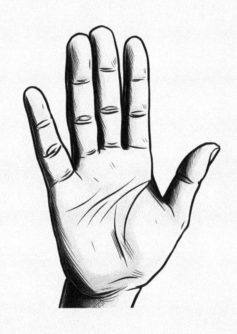

You should stop here.

Do not turn the page.

OK, so you turned the page, but I'm

Seri

ous!

I don't think you will
ever finish this book.

It's just too **complicated**.

The ideas are too big and too important
for anyone to ever truly understand.

Are you **really sure** you want to read it?

Really?!

If you read this book, it might change **everything about you.**

Still here?

You asked for it...

Turn the page if you're ready to start your journey. ————‹‹‹‹

Have you ever **tried** to do something so hard you didn't think you could ever, ever do it?

I mean really, really, *really*, hard.

Maybe something **physically hard**, like playing a new instrument.

Or something **emotionally hard**, like having no one to take care of you.

Or maybe **mentally hard**, like not understanding what is going on around you, or encountering something that scares you.

What did you do?

Give up?

Get angry?

Feel sorry for yourself?

**Believe you're not smart enough...
or good enough?**

Any guesses what happens when we choose *not* to do hard things?

Hooray!

You get to do the easy thing!

There can be more time for
TV, video games, and fun!!!

And maybe doing the
easy thing feels great.

But, dear reader...

I told you this book
wasn't going to be easy.

Let me tell you a very **special secret** most people don't know.

Doing the hard thing will
eventually turn you into a...

RO.

Yup, that's right!

Can you guess what makes a hero?

Heroes are **kind**.

Heroes are **generous**.

Heroes **help** other people.

Heroes **face danger*** even when they're afraid.

Heroes do everything for a **reason** and with **purpose**.

*Dear reader, until you are a grownup, never face danger on your own!

A hero doesn't care what the villain—
or anyone else—thinks about them.

A hero never looks outward for approval, but chooses their own value for themselves.

Think about all the heroes you love!

Whether they are big or small, clever or strong, we watch them overcome something that seems impossible and

HARD.

If it was easy, would they still be heroes?

When was the last time you saw a hero
you loved only do something easy?

What does that tell us about **hard things?**

When we face hard things, it transforms us.

Like...

Facing a mean bully.

Learning to play an instrument.

Understanding a difficult math problem.

Making new friends.

Watching someone you love, die.

None of these things are easy.

But whoever said becoming a hero was going to be easy?

I promise, you didn't hear that from me!

Every good wonderful life waits other side

and
thing in
on the
of HARD.

A hero becomes a hero only when
they get to the **other side of HARD.**

Like when they defeat the villain, save the world, or think they can't win, try anyway, and then succeed!

Especially when it seems absolutely and completely impossible!

And most of all, heroes try **even when they're afraid.**

Wow,

you're almost done with this book!

I warned you about reading this book and you decided to do it anyway.

Can you feel yourself changing and transforming into something great?

Sometimes, doing the hard thing will launch you into the greatest adventure of your life.

But you have to choose it.

Just like I did...

W
hen I was young, my parents weren't around to care for me.

I felt completely abandoned.

I was raised by strangers who didn't like me or treat me very well.

By high school, I could barely write and didn't know any math. None.

I felt like everything I did was wrong.

And I felt like this for years.

Until one day...

I got an invitation to an entirely new life, where I would be taken care of, fed, clothed, and educated. I couldn't believe it.

And I said**...no.**

I was too afraid and ashamed of what I didn't know.

But after a while, I knew I needed a change and was finally ready to choose.

And when I did, **my whole life changed.**

I learned to write.

I learned math.

It was hard, but it was so good.

And before I knew it, I was on my way to England...to one of the **best universities in the world!**

Poverty. Abandonment.
Illiteracy. Manipulation.

That's the beginning of my story.
It may not be your story.

But you have your
own story to share.

About when you did or went
through something hard—and
made it to the other side.

What's hard for you, *is* HARD.

And everyone's HARD looks different.

Whether you know it or not,
you might be living your hard right now.

Dearest reader, please know you don't need to go through your hard alone. If you are mistreated by those who should be caring for you, like I was, please talk to a trusted grownup to get help.

If you've lost someone you've loved and still watch movies and eat french fries, **you've done something hard.**

If you've tried out for a team and didn't make it, **you've done something hard.**

If you've been treated badly by others, **you've done something hard.**

The hard things you've done have made you who you are.

You are stronger, smarter, and more powerful because you've done what's hard.

So when you encounter something hard...

Don't run from it.

Run towards it.

Because no matter what your hard is, once you do it, **you will never be the same.**

You will have good days
and bad days.

But just remember,
if you choose hard things, then...

YOU ARE A HERO!

Outro

Completing an impossible quest or conquering an adversary you think you can't defeat just might be one of the most important things you choose to do.

No matter what hard thing you face in life, you get to choose how you look at it. You can choose to give up or decide you are too afraid to try. Or, you can choose the hero's path and forge ahead, despite the doubts or fears you feel.

When you choose to accomplish or overcome the impossible, you choose to see yourself and your life as a magical quest. When you make this very important choice, you will find that you can do far more than you ever thought yourself capable of. And, you will come out stronger and more powerful, just like your greatest heroes.

About The Author

Jamie Mustard (he/him) is an artist and multi-award-winning writer who loves to reverse-engineer things. He learned to do this growing up in poverty and abandonment. He finds patterns in everything around him, and he makes connections that others might not see. Then, he talks about them in a way anyone can understand. It's his superpower.

He wrote his first 2 books to inspire others. *The Iconist* was written to help others stand out in a world experiencing mass-messaging overload. He co-wrote his second book, *The Invisible Machine*, with a famous scientist who figured out how to make life better for those who go through difficult quests in their lives.

Superpowers should help others, and Jamie shares his powers so that others won't have to experience the invisibility he felt as a kid. Jamie believes that when we choose to frame our lives as a quest rather than a disaster, eventually, anyone can do the impossible.

@jamie_mustard   jamie-mustard-872b283/

a kids book about
MONEY
Strawasser

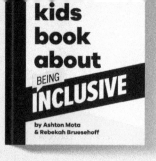
a kids book about
BEING
INCLUSIVE
by Ashton Mota
& Rebekah Bruesehoff

a kids book about
diversity

a kids book about
LEADERSHIP
by Orion Jean

a kids book about
IMMIG
by MJ Calder

a kids book about
SAFETY
by Soraya Sutherlin, CEM
in partnership with JUDY

a kids book about
CLIMATE CHANGE
by Zanagee Artis
Olivia Greenspan

a kids book about
IMAGINATION
by LEVAR BURTON

a kids book about
CONFIDENCE
by Joy Cho

a ki
boo
ab
B

kids ok out
Opecia
n Van

a kids book about
NEURO-DIVERSITY
by Laura Petix, MS OTR/L

a kids book about
racism
by Jelani Memory

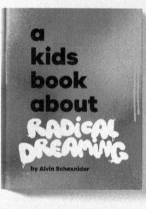
a kids book about
RADICAL DREAMING
by Alvin Schexnider

a kids book about
bor
by: KYLES

a kids book about
DIVORCE
by Ashley Simpo

a kids book about
EQUALITY
by BILLIE JEAN KING

a kids book about
CONSENT
by Karli Johnson

a kids book about
PRIDE
by Kendall Clawson

c
k
k
by

ds ok out ame

a kids book about
BLENDED FAMILIES

Discover more at akidsco.com

Printed in the USA
CPSIA information can be obtained
at www.ICGtesting.com
LVHW060826261223
767352LV00014B/1205